Teen Witch's
Book of Shadows

Spellcaster's Magickal Recipes

Katharine Rose

Brock Haus Press

Teen Witch's Book of Shadows: Spellcaster's Magickal Recipes | Katharine Rose
ISBN: 978-1-7324279-8-3

What is a Book of Shadows?

Track your spells, rituals, and other things related to your development as a witch. It's like a chef's collection of recipes. Record your musings and insights related to your spells, as well as your dreams, feelings and other asides. This Book of Shadows records sixty spells or rituals consisting of a two-page journal entry to record your magickal recipes and personal experiences. The last journal pages you may record a snapshot of your dates of castings and manifestations.

So mote it be!

Spells & Rituals

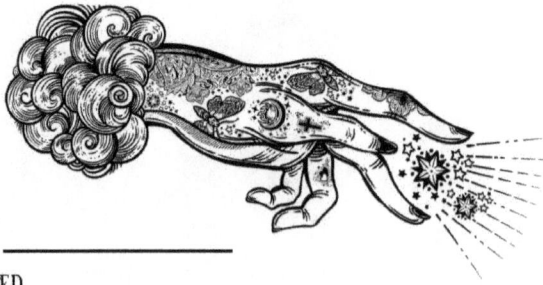

DATE _____

CASTER _____

RITUAL OR SPELL _____

PURPOSE _____

PARTICIPANTS _____

DEITIES INVOLVED _____

MANIFESTATION DATE _____

MOON PHASE _____

DESCRIPTION

FEELINGS & EFFECTS

INGREDIENTS & EQUIPMENT

_____

_____

_____

_____

_____

"So Mote It Be"

NoTES

NoTES

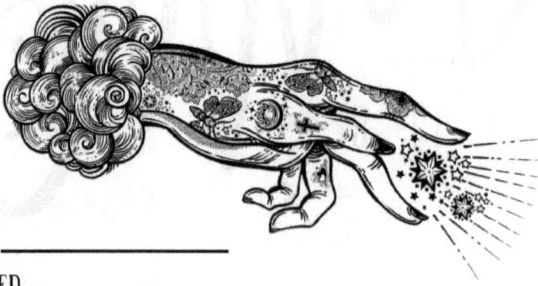

DATE _____

CASTER _____

RITUAL OR SPELL _____

PURPOSE _____

PARTICIPANTS _____

DEITIES INVOLVED _____

MANIFESTATION DATE _____

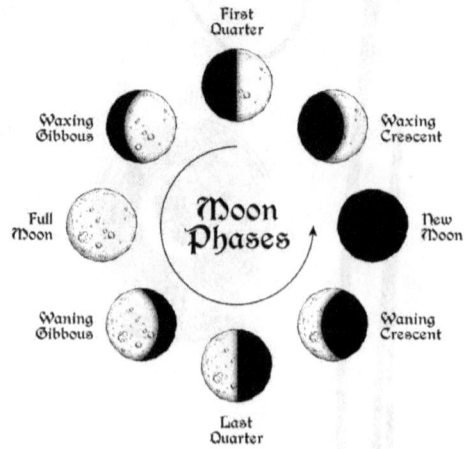

MOON PHASE _____

DESCRIPTION

FEELINGS & EFFECTS

INGREDIENTS & EQUIPMENT

_____

_____

_____

_____

_____

"SO MOTE IT BE"

NOTES

NOTES

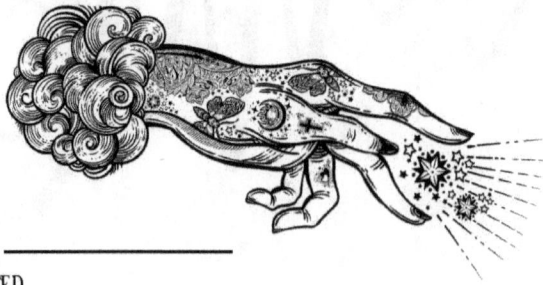

DATE _____

CASTER _____

RITUAL OR SPELL _____

PURPOSE _____

PARTICIPANTS _____

DEITIES INVOLVED _____

MANIFESTATION DATE _____

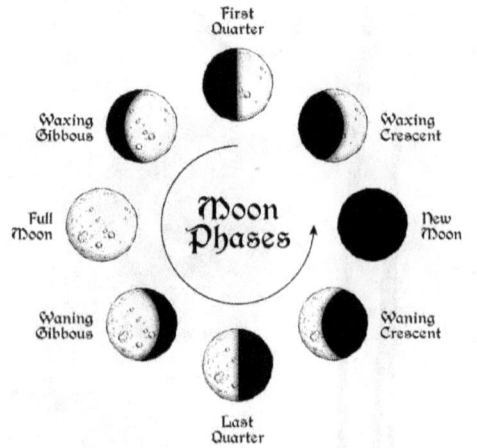

MOON PHASE _____

DESCRIPTION

FEELINGS & EFFECTS

INGREDIENTS & EQUIPMENT

_____

_____

_____

_____

_____

"So Mote It Be"

NOTES

NOTES

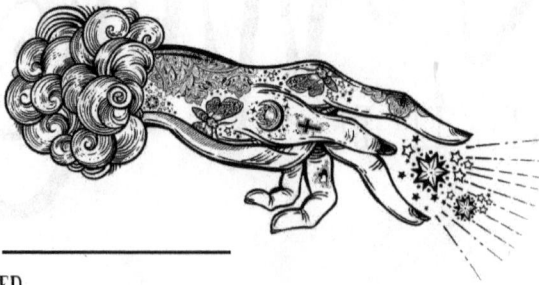

DATE _____

CASTER _____

RITUAL OR SPELL _____

PURPOSE _____

PARTICIPANTS _____

DEITIES INVOLVED _____

MANIFESTATION DATE _____

MOON PHASE _____

DESCRIPTION

FEELINGS & EFFECTS

INGREDIENTS & EQUIPMENT

_____

_____

_____

_____

_____

"So Mote It Be"

NoTES

NoTES

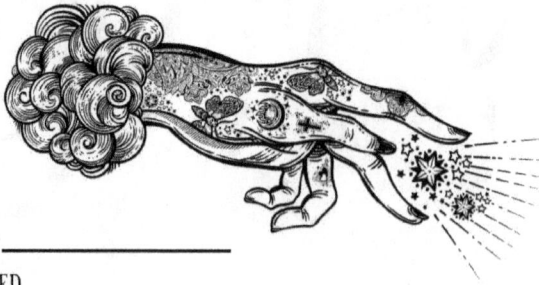

DATE _____

CASTER _____

RITUAL OR SPELL _____

PURPOSE _____

PARTICIPANTS _____

DEITIES INVOLVED _____

MANIFESTATION DATE _____

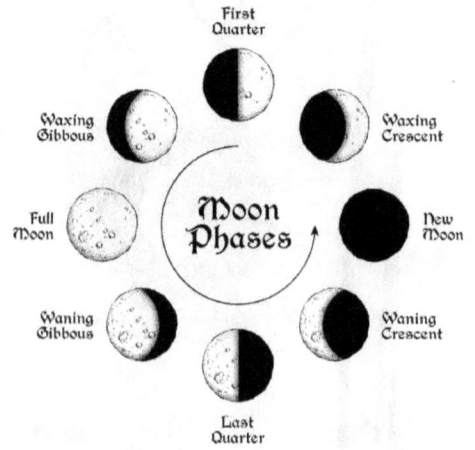

MOON PHASE _____

DESCRIPTION

FEELINGS & EFFECTS

INGREDIENTS & EQUIPMENT

_____

_____

_____

_____

_____

_____

"So Mote It Be"

NOTES

NOTES

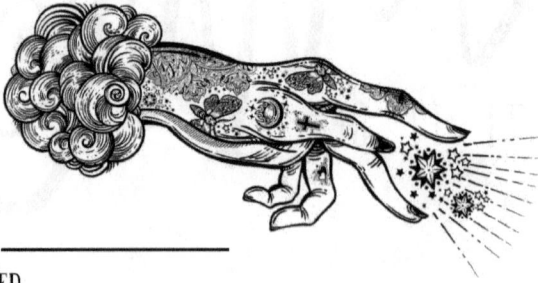

DATE _____

CASTER _____

RITUAL OR SPELL _____

PURPOSE _____

PARTICIPANTS _____

DEITIES INVOLVED _____

MANIFESTATION DATE _____

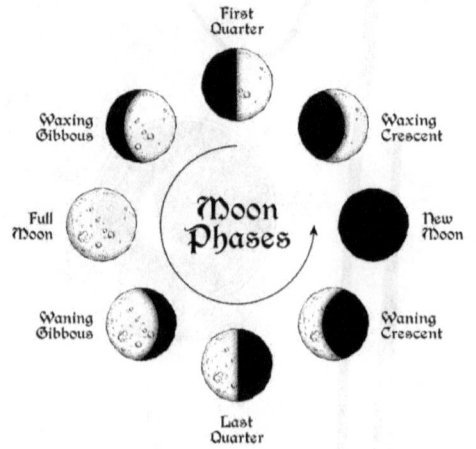

MOON PHASE _____

DESCRIPTION

FEELINGS & EFFECTS

INGREDIENTS & EQUIPMENT

_____

_____

_____

_____

_____

"So Mote it Be"

NOTES

NOTES

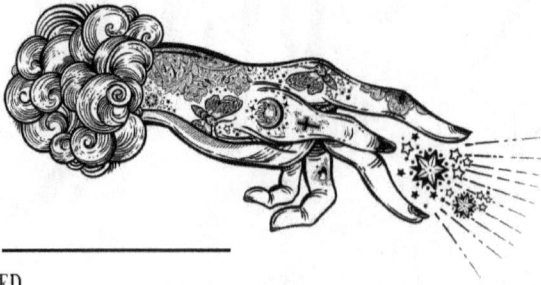

DATE _____

CASTER _____

RITUAL oR SPELL _____

PURPoSE _____

PARTICIPANTS _____

DEITIES INVOLVED _____

MANIFESTATION DATE _____

MooN PHASE _____

DESCRIPTION

FEELINGS & EFFECTS

INGREDIENTS & EQUIPMENT

"So Mote It Be"

NoTES

NoTES

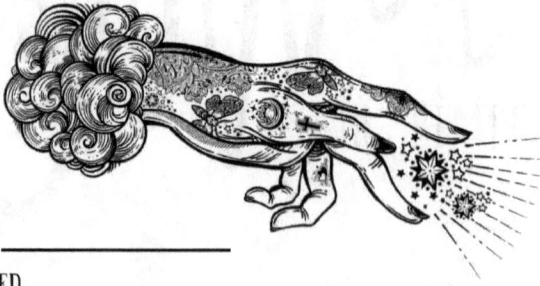

DATE _____

CASTER _____

RITUAL OR SPELL _____

PURPOSE _____

PARTICIPANTS _____

DEITIES INVOLVED _____

MANIFESTATION DATE _____

MOON PHASE _____

DESCRIPTION

FEELINGS & EFFECTS

INGREDIENTS & EQUIPMENT

_____

_____

_____

_____

_____

"So Mote It Be"

NOTES

NOTES

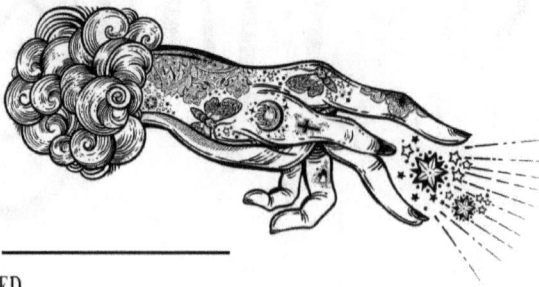

DATE _____

CASTER _____

RITUAL OR SPELL _____

PURPOSE _____

PARTICIPANTS _____

DEITIES INVOLVED _____

MANIFESTATION DATE _____

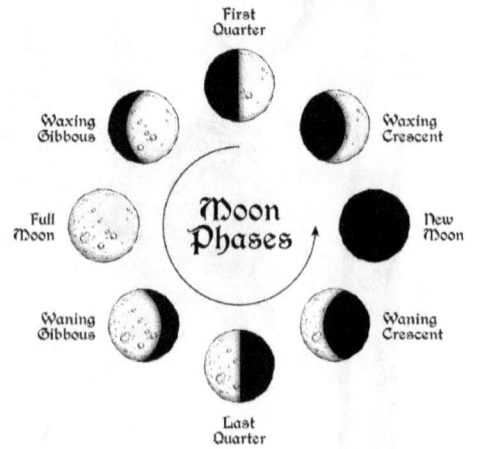

MOON PHASE _____

DESCRIPTION

FEELINGS & EFFECTS

INGREDIENTS & EQUIPMENT

"SO MOTE IT BE"

NOTES

NOTES

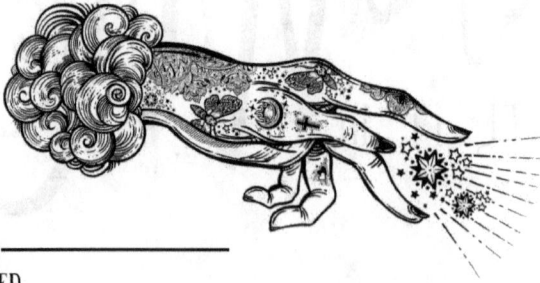

DATE _____

CASTER _____

RITUAL OR SPELL _____

PURPOSE _____

PARTICIPANTS _____

DEITIES INVOLVED _____

MANIFESTATION DATE _____

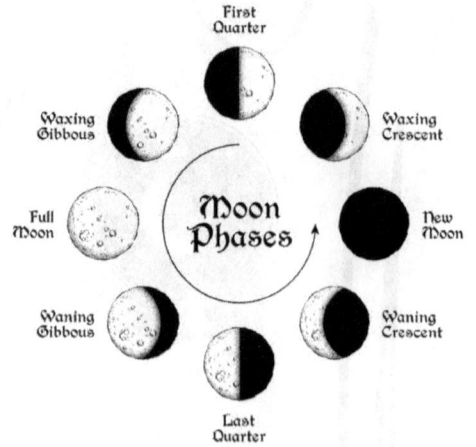

Moon Phases

First Quarter
Waxing Gibbous
Waxing Crescent
Full Moon
New Moon
Waning Gibbous
Waning Crescent
Last Quarter

MOON PHASE _____

DESCRIPTION

FEELINGS & EFFECTS

INGREDIENTS & EQUIPMENT

_____

_____

_____

_____

_____

"So Mote It Be"

NOTES

NOTES

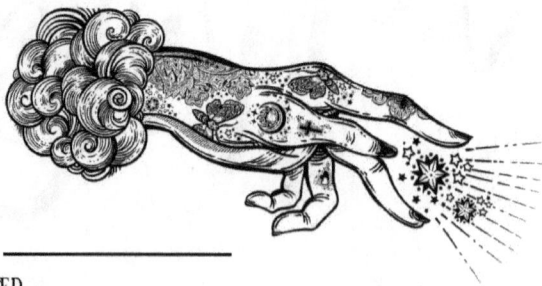

DATE _____

CASTER _____

RITUAL OR SPELL _____

PURPOSE _____

PARTICIPANTS _____

DEITIES INVOLVED _____

MANIFESTATION DATE _____

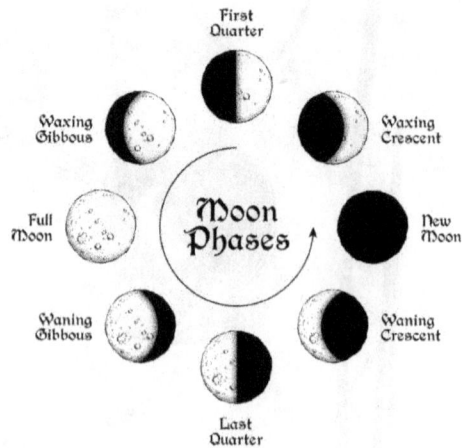

First
Quarter

Waxing
Gibbous

Waxing
Crescent

Full
Moon

Moon
Phases

New
Moon

Waning
Gibbous

Waning
Crescent

Last
Quarter

MOON PHASE _____

DESCRIPTION

FEELINGS & EFFECTS

INGREDIENTS & EQUIPMENT

_____

_____

_____

_____

_____

_____

"So Mote it Be"

NOTES

NOTES

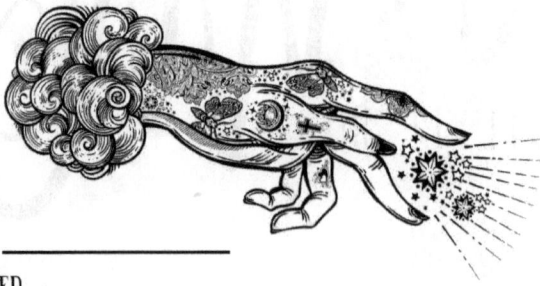

DATE _____

CASTER _____

RITUAL oR SPELL _____

PURPoSE _____

PARTICIPANTS _____

DEITIES INVoLVED _____

MANIFESTATION DATE _____

MOoN PHASE _____

DESCRIPTION

FEELINGS & EFFECTS

INGREDIENTS & EQUIPMENT

"So Mote It Be"

NoTES

NoTES

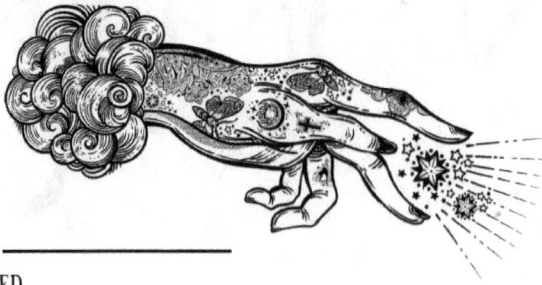

DATE _____

CASTER _____

RITUAL OR SPELL _____

PURPOSE _____

PARTICIPANTS _____

DEITIES INVOLVED _____

MANIFESTATION DATE _____

MOON PHASE _____

DESCRIPTION

FEELINGS & EFFECTS

INGREDIENTS & EQUIPMENT

_____

_____

_____

_____

_____

"So Mote It Be"

NOTES

NOTES

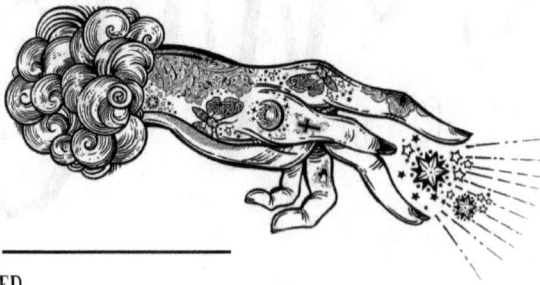

DATE _____

CASTER _____

RITUAL OR SPELL _____

PURPOSE _____

PARTICIPANTS _____

DEITIES INVOLVED _____

MANIFESTATION DATE _____

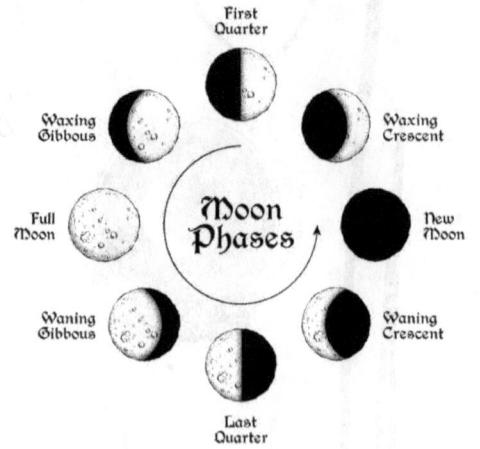

MOON PHASE _____

DESCRIPTION

FEELINGS & EFFECTS

INGREDIENTS & EQUIPMENT

_____

_____

_____

_____

_____

"So Mote It Be"

NOTES

NOTES

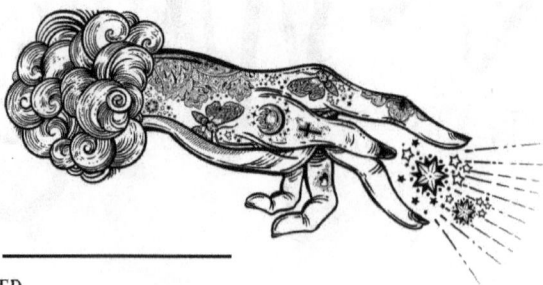

DATE _____

CASTER _____

RITUAL OR SPELL _____

PURPOSE _____

PARTICIPANTS _____

DEITIES INVOLVED _____

MANIFESTATION DATE _____

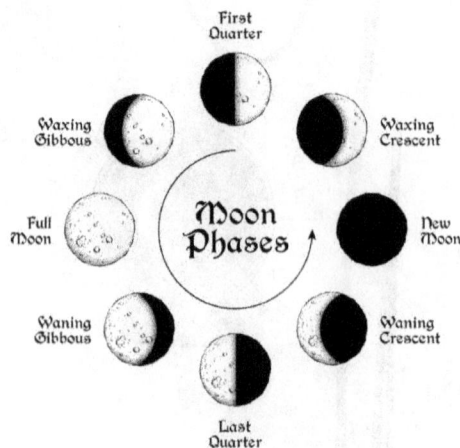

MOON PHASE _____

DESCRIPTION

FEELINGS & EFFECTS

INGREDIENTS & EQUIPMENT

"So Mote it Be"

NoTES

NoTES

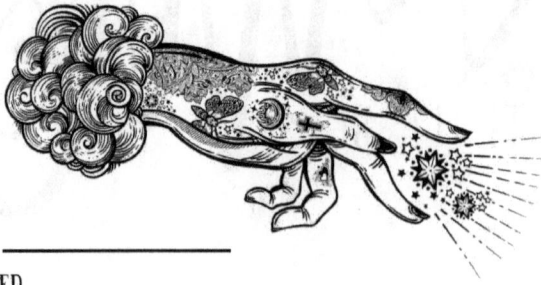

DATE _____

CASTER _____

RITUAL OR SPELL _____

PURPOSE _____

PARTICIPANTS _____

DEITIES INVOLVED _____

MANIFESTATION DATE _____

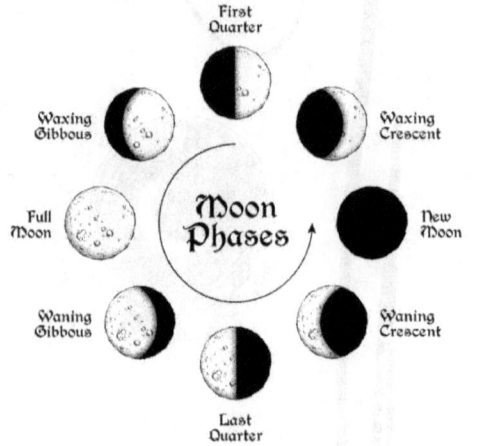

MOON PHASE _____

DESCRIPTION

INGREDIENTS & EQUIPMENT

_____

_____

_____

_____

_____

FEELINGS & EFFECTS

"So Mote It Be"

NoTES

NoTES

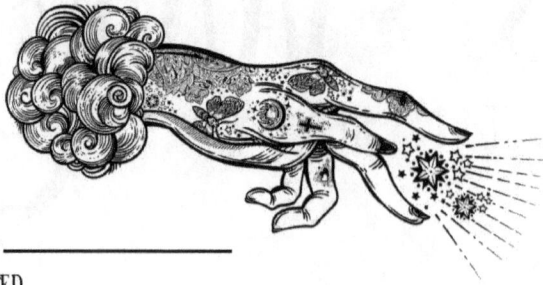

DATE _____

CASTER _____

RITUAL OR SPELL _____

PURPOSE _____

PARTICIPANTS _____

DEITIES INVOLVED _____

MANIFESTATION DATE _____

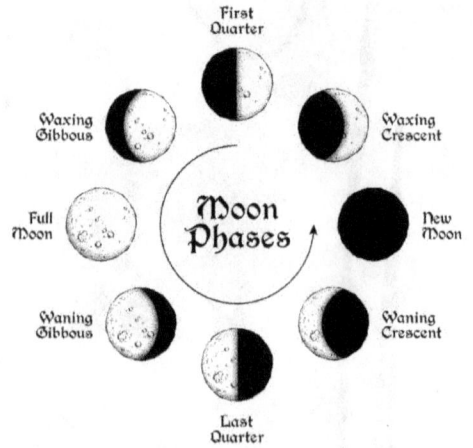

MOON PHASE _____

DESCRIPTION

FEELINGS & EFFECTS

INGREDIENTS & EQUIPMENT

"SO MOTE IT BE"

NOTES

NOTES

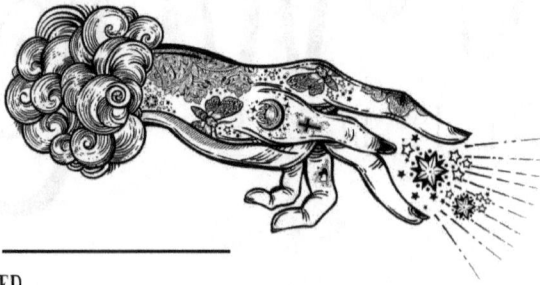

DATE _____

CASTER _____

RITUAL OR SPELL _____

PURPOSE _____

PARTICIPANTS _____

DEITIES INVOLVED _____

MANIFESTATION DATE _____

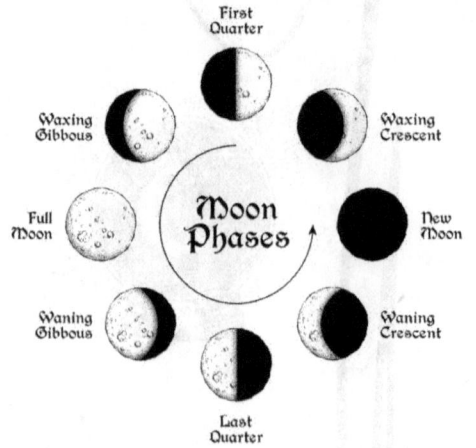

MOON PHASE _____

DESCRIPTION

FEELINGS & EFFECTS

INGREDIENTS & EQUIPMENT

_____

_____

_____

_____

_____

"So Mote It Be"

NoTES

NoTES

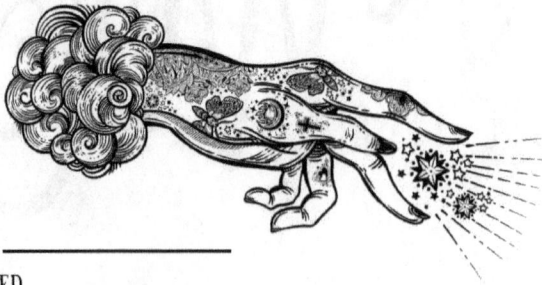

DATE _____

CASTER _____

RITUAL OR SPELL _____

PURPOSE _____

PARTICIPANTS _____

DEITIES INVOLVED _____

MANIFESTATION DATE _____

MOON PHASE _____

DESCRIPTION

FEELINGS & EFFECTS

INGREDIENTS & EQUIPMENT

_____

_____

_____

_____

_____

_____

"So Mote It Be"

NOTES

NOTES

Dream

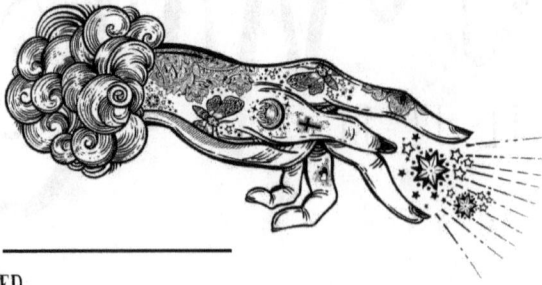

DATE _____

CASTER _____

RITUAL OR SPELL _____

PURPOSE _____

PARTICIPANTS _____

DEITIES INVOLVED _____

MANIFESTATION DATE _____

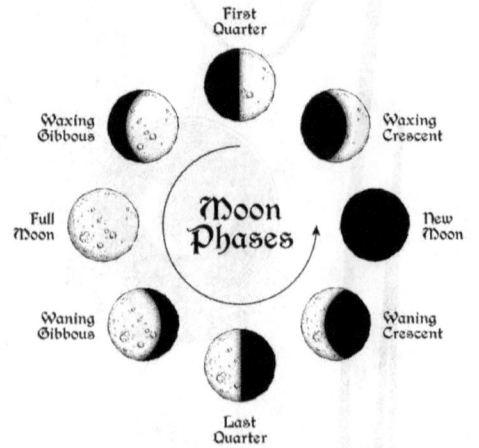

MOON PHASE _____

DESCRIPTION

FEELINGS & EFFECTS

INGREDIENTS & EQUIPMENT

_____

_____

_____

_____

_____

"SO MOTE IT BE"

NOTES

NOTES

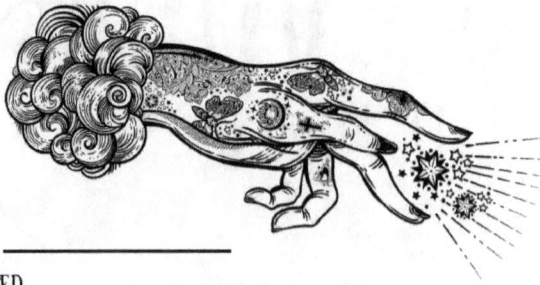

DATE _____

CASTER _____

RITUAL OR SPELL _____

PURPOSE _____

PARTICIPANTS _____

DEITIES INVOLVED _____

MANIFESTATION DATE _____

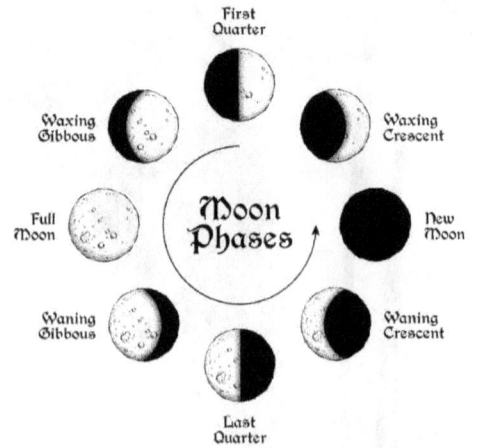

MOON PHASE _____

DESCRIPTION

FEELINGS & EFFECTS

INGREDIENTS & EQUIPMENT

_____

_____

_____

_____

_____

_____

"SO MOTE IT BE"

NOTES

NOTES

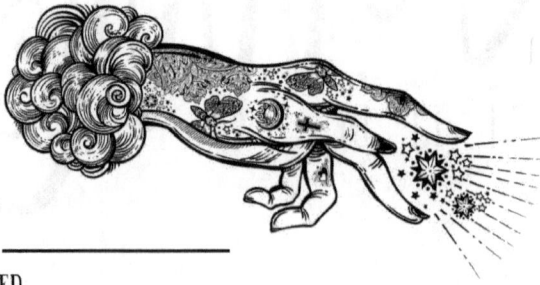

DATE _____

CASTER _____

RITUAL OR SPELL _____

PURPOSE _____

PARTICIPANTS _____

DEITIES INVOLVED _____

MANIFESTATION DATE _____

MOON PHASE _____

DESCRIPTION

FEELINGS & EFFECTS

INGREDIENTS & EQUIPMENT

"So Mote It Be"

NOTES

NOTES

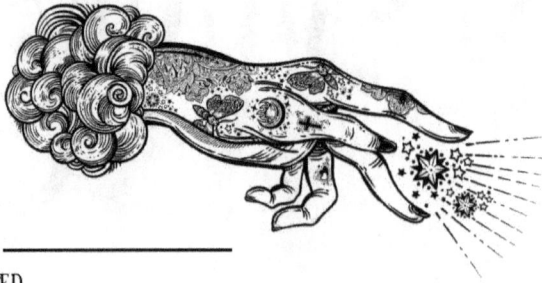

DATE _____

CASTER _____

RITUAL OR SPELL _____

PURPOSE _____

PARTICIPANTS _____

DEITIES INVOLVED _____

MANIFESTATION DATE _____

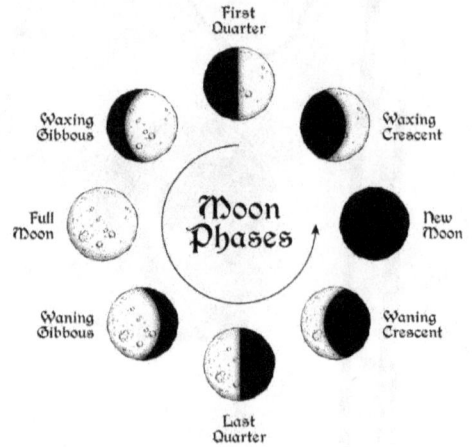

MOON PHASE _____

DESCRIPTION

FEELINGS & EFFECTS

INGREDIENTS & EQUIPMENT

_____

_____

_____

_____

_____

_____

"So Mote it be"

NOTES

NOTES

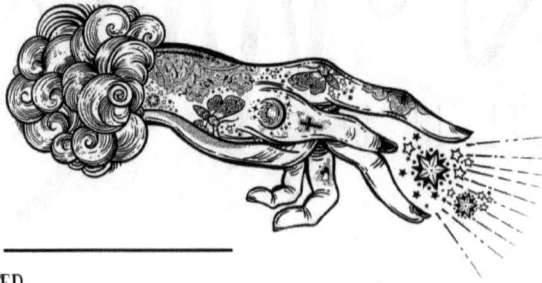

DATE _____

CASTER _____

RITUAL OR SPELL _____

PURPOSE _____

PARTICIPANTS _____

DEITIES INVOLVED _____

MANIFESTATION DATE _____

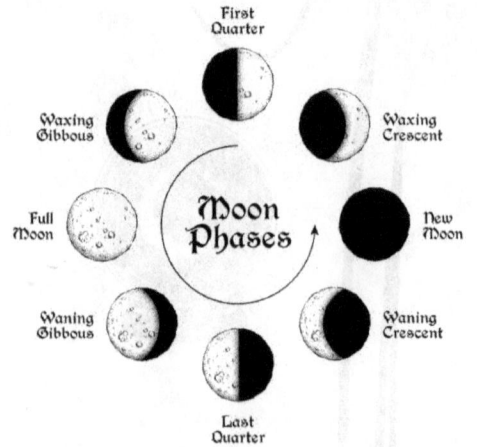

MOON PHASE _____

DESCRIPTION

FEELINGS & EFFECTS

INGREDIENTS & EQUIPMENT

_____

_____

_____

_____

_____

"SO MOTE IT BE"

NOTES

NOTES

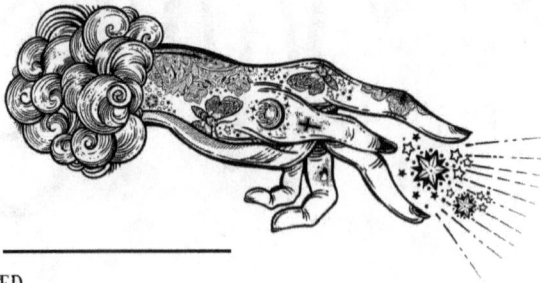

DATE _____

CASTER _____

RITUAL OR SPELL _____

PURPOSE _____

PARTICIPANTS _____

DEITIES INVOLVED _____

MANIFESTATION DATE _____

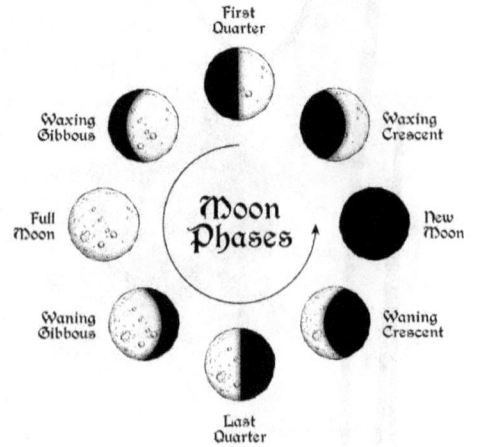

MOON PHASE _____

DESCRIPTION

INGREDIENTS & EQUIPMENT

_____

_____

_____

_____

_____

_____

FEELINGS & EFFECTS

"So Mote It Be"

NOTES

NOTES

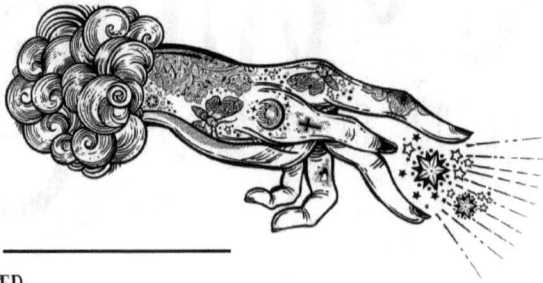

DATE _____

CASTER _____

RITUAL oR SPELL _____

PURPoSE _____

PARTICIPANTS _____

DEITIES INVoLVED _____

MANIFESTATION DATE _____

First Quarter

Waxing Gibbous

Waxing Crescent

Full Moon

Moon Phases

New Moon

Waning Gibbous

Waning Crescent

Last Quarter

MooN PHASE _____

DESCRIPTION

FEELINGS & EFFECTS

INGREDIENTS & EQUIPMENT

_____

_____

_____

_____

_____

_____

"So Mote It Be"

NOTES

NOTES

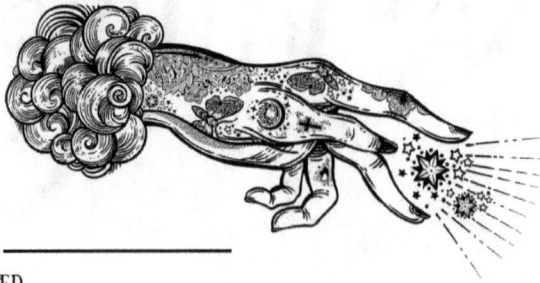

DATE _____

CASTER _____

RITUAL OR SPELL _____

PURPOSE _____

PARTICIPANTS _____

DEITIES INVOLVED _____

MANIFESTATION DATE _____

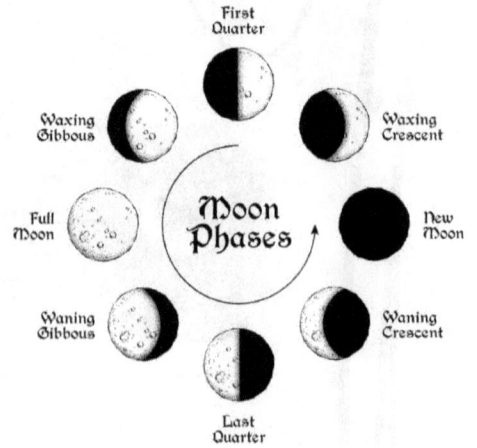

MOON PHASE _____

DESCRIPTION

FEELINGS & EFFECTS

INGREDIENTS & EQUIPMENT

_____

_____

_____

_____

_____

_____

"So Mote It Be"

NOTES

NOTES

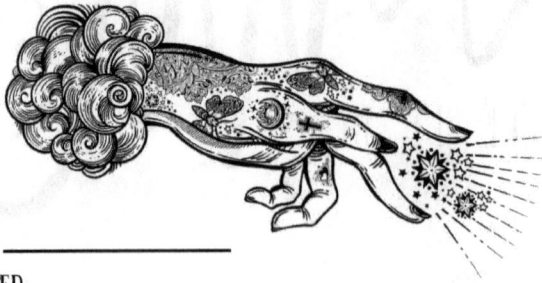

DATE _____

CASTER _____

RITUAL OR SPELL _____

PURPOSE _____

PARTICIPANTS _____

DEITIES INVOLVED _____

MANIFESTATION DATE _____

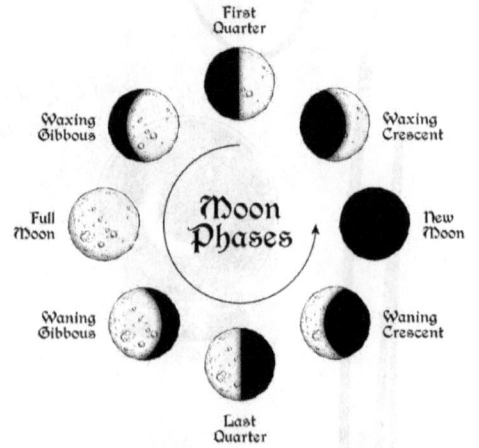

MOON PHASE _____

DESCRIPTION

FEELINGS & EFFECTS

INGREDIENTS & EQUIPMENT

_____

_____

_____

_____

_____

_____

"So Mote It Be"

NOTES

NOTES

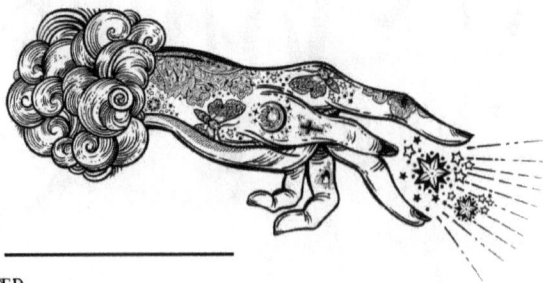

DATE _____

CASTER _____

RITUAL OR SPELL _____

PURPOSE _____

PARTICIPANTS _____

DEITIES INVOLVED _____

MANIFESTATION DATE _____

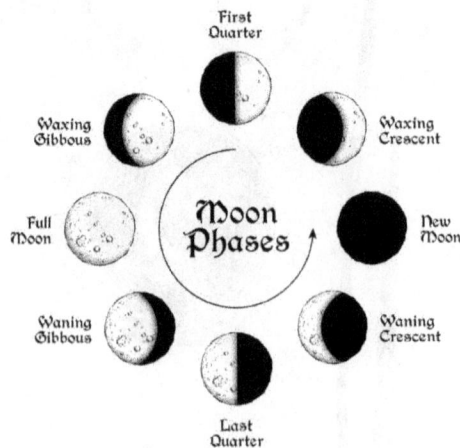

MOON PHASE _____

DESCRIPTION

FEELINGS & EFFECTS

INGREDIENTS & EQUIPMENT

_____

_____

_____

_____

_____

"SO MOTE IT BE"

NOTES

NOTES

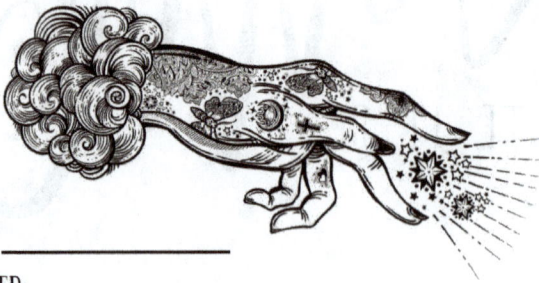

DATE _____

CASTER _____

RITUAL OR SPELL _____

PURPOSE _____

PARTICIPANTS _____

DEITIES INVOLVED _____

MANIFESTATION DATE _____

MOON PHASE _____

DESCRIPTION

FEELINGS & EFFECTS

INGREDIENTS & EQUIPMENT

"So Mote It Be"

NoTES

NoTES

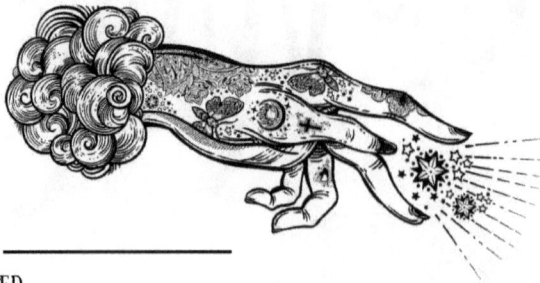

DATE _____

CASTER _____

RITUAL OR SPELL _____

PURPOSE _____

PARTICIPANTS _____

DEITIES INVOLVED _____

MANIFESTATION DATE _____

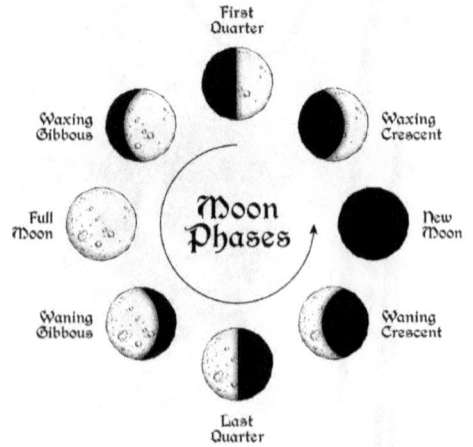

MOON PHASE _____

DESCRIPTION

FEELINGS & EFFECTS

INGREDIENTS & EQUIPMENT

_____

_____

_____

_____

_____

_____

"So Mote It Be"

NoTES

NoTES

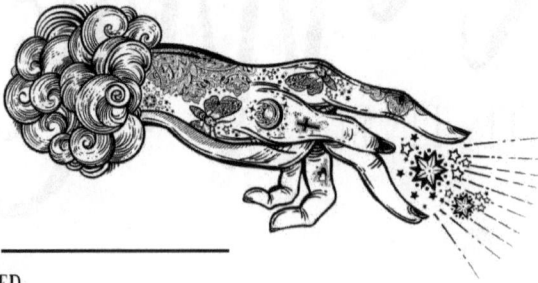

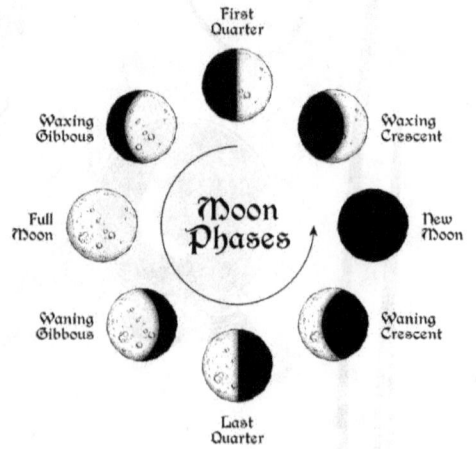

DATE _____

CASTER _____

RITUAL OR SPELL _____

PURPOSE _____

PARTICIPANTS _____

DEITIES INVOLVED _____

MANIFESTATION DATE _____

MOON PHASE _____

DESCRIPTION

FEELINGS & EFFECTS

INGREDIENTS & EQUIPMENT

_____

_____

_____

_____

_____

_____

"So Mote It Be"

NOTES

NOTES

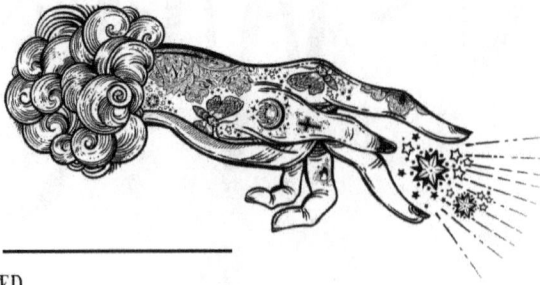

DATE _____

CASTER _____

RITUAL OR SPELL _____

PURPOSE _____

PARTICIPANTS _____

DEITIES INVOLVED _____

MANIFESTATION DATE _____

MOON PHASE _____

DESCRIPTION

FEELINGS & EFFECTS

INGREDIENTS & EQUIPMENT

_____

_____

_____

_____

_____

_____

"So Mote it be"

NOTES

NOTES

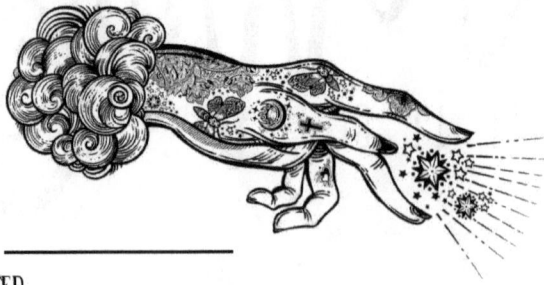

DATE _____

CASTER _____

RITUAL OR SPELL _____

PURPOSE _____

PARTICIPANTS _____

DEITIES INVOLVED _____

MANIFESTATION DATE _____

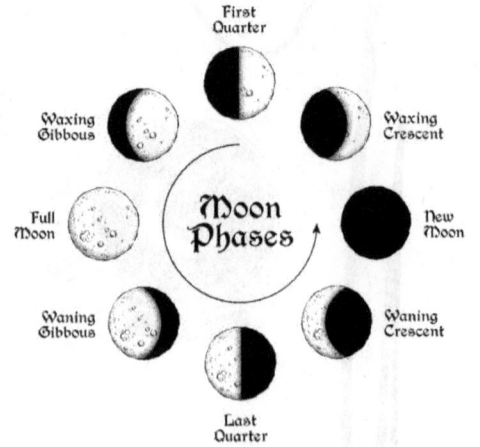

MOON PHASE _____

DESCRIPTION

FEELINGS & EFFECTS

INGREDIENTS & EQUIPMENT

_____

_____

_____

_____

_____

_____

"So Mote It Be"

NOTES

NOTES

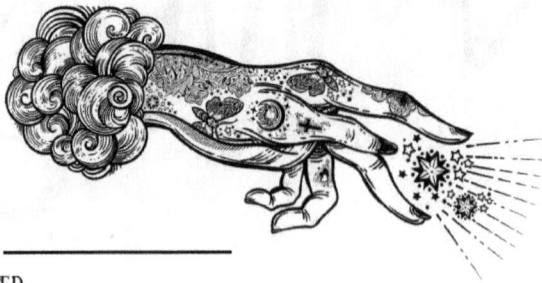

DATE _____

CASTER _____

RITUAL OR SPELL _____

PURPOSE _____

PARTICIPANTS _____

DEITIES INVOLVED _____

MANIFESTATION DATE _____

MOON PHASE _____

DESCRIPTION

FEELINGS & EFFECTS

INGREDIENTS & EQUIPMENT

_____

_____

_____

_____

_____

_____

"So Mote It Be"

NoTES

NoTES

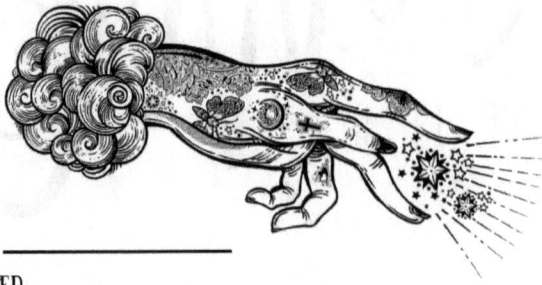

DATE _____

CASTER _____

RITUAL OR SPELL _____

PURPOSE _____

PARTICIPANTS _____

DEITIES INVOLVED _____

MANIFESTATION DATE _____

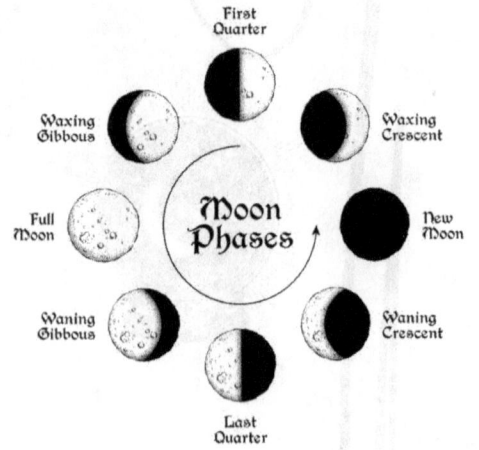

MOON PHASE _____

DESCRIPTION

FEELINGS & EFFECTS

INGREDIENTS & EQUIPMENT

"SO MOTE IT BE"

NOTES

NOTES

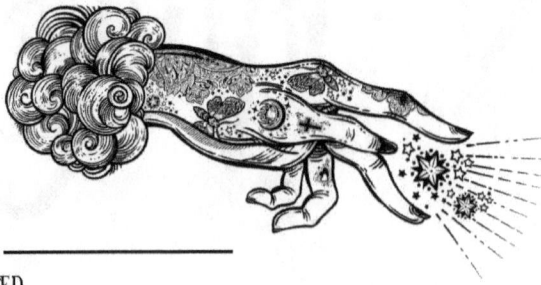

DATE _____

CASTER _____

RITUAL oR SPELL _____

PURPoSE _____

PARTICIPANTS _____

DEITIES INVoLVED _____

MANIFESTATION DATE _____

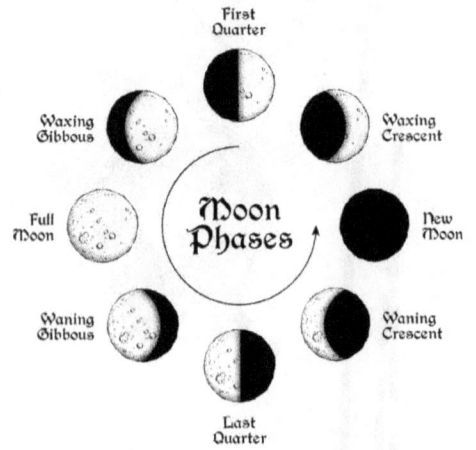

MOON PHASE _____

DESCRIPTION

INGREDIENTS & EQUIPMENT

_____

_____

_____

_____

_____

_____

FEELINGS & EFFECTS

"So Mote it be"

NOTES

NOTES

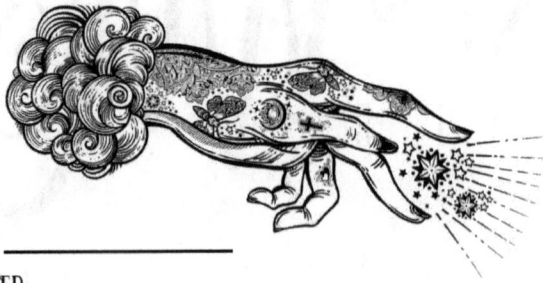

DATE _____

CASTER _____

RITUAL OR SPELL _____

PURPOSE _____

PARTICIPANTS _____

DEITIES INVOLVED _____

MANIFESTATION DATE _____

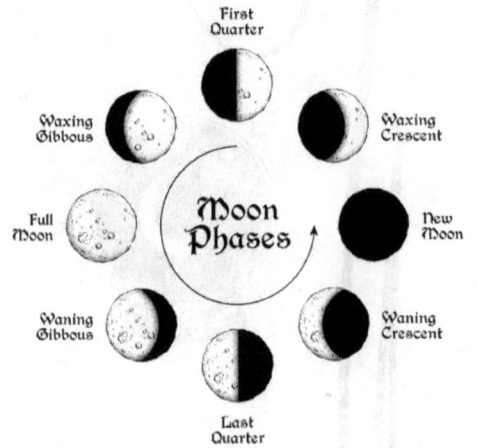

MOON PHASE _____

DESCRIPTION

FEELINGS & EFFECTS

INGREDIENTS & EQUIPMENT

"So Mote it be"

NOTES

NOTES

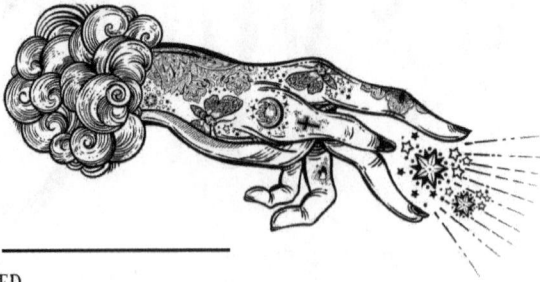

DATE _____

CASTER _____

RITUAL OR SPELL _____

PURPOSE _____

PARTICIPANTS _____

DEITIES INVOLVED _____

MANIFESTATION DATE _____

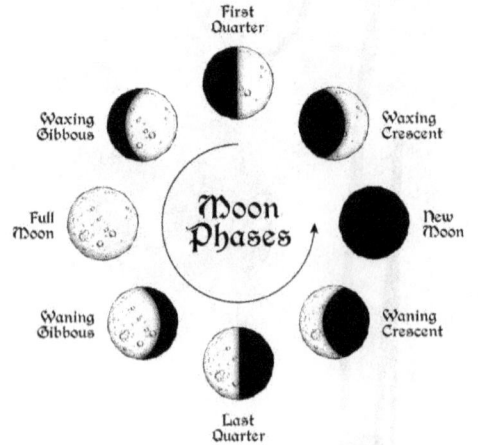

First
Quarter

Waxing
Gibbous

Waxing
Crescent

Full
Moon

Moon Phases

New
Moon

Waning
Gibbous

Waning
Crescent

Last
Quarter

MOON PHASE _____

DESCRIPTION

FEELINGS & EFFECTS

INGREDIENTS & EQUIPMENT

"So Mote It Be"

NoTES

NoTES

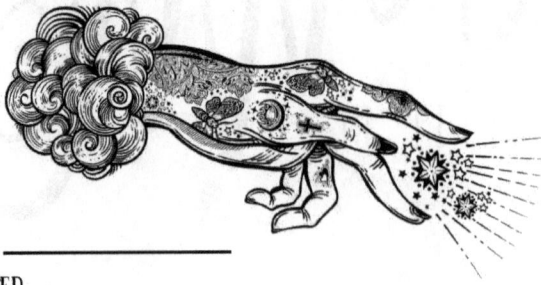

DATE _____

CASTER _____

RITUAL OR SPELL _____

PURPOSE _____

PARTICIPANTS _____

DEITIES INVOLVED _____

MANIFESTATION DATE _____

MOON PHASE _____

DESCRIPTION

FEELINGS & EFFECTS

INGREDIENTS & EQUIPMENT

_____

_____

_____

_____

_____

"So Mote It Be"

NOTES

NOTES

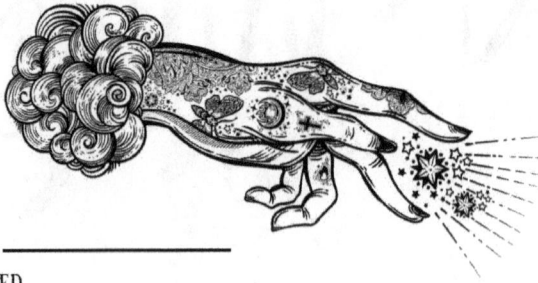

DATE _____

CASTER _____

RITUAL OR SPELL _____

PURPOSE _____

PARTICIPANTS _____

DEITIES INVOLVED _____

MANIFESTATION DATE _____

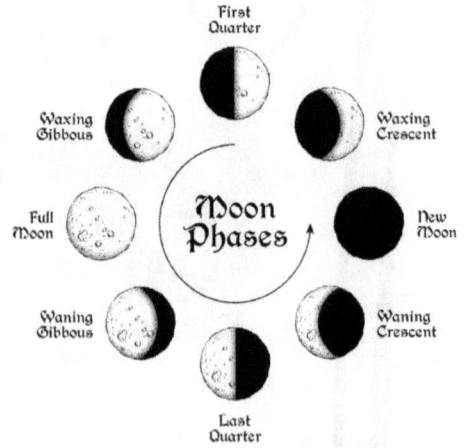

MOON PHASE _____

DESCRIPTION

FEELINGS & EFFECTS

INGREDIENTS & EQUIPMENT

_____

_____

_____

_____

_____

"So Mote It Be"

NOTES

NOTES

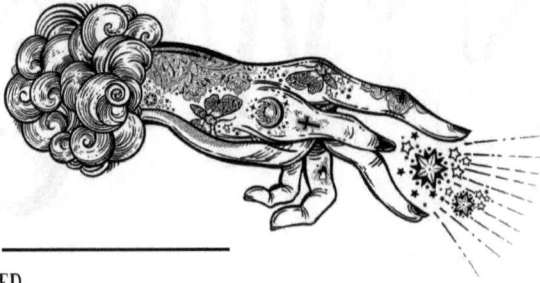

DATE _____

CASTER _____

RITUAL OR SPELL _____

PURPOSE _____

PARTICIPANTS _____

DEITIES INVOLVED _____

MANIFESTATION DATE _____

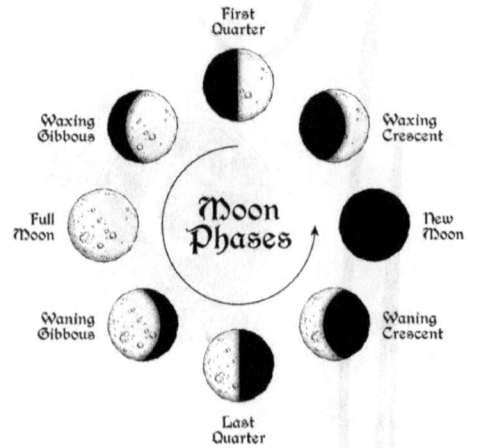

MOON PHASE _____

DESCRIPTION

FEELINGS & EFFECTS

INGREDIENTS & EQUIPMENT

_____

_____

_____

_____

_____

_____

"So Mote It Be"

NOTES

NOTES

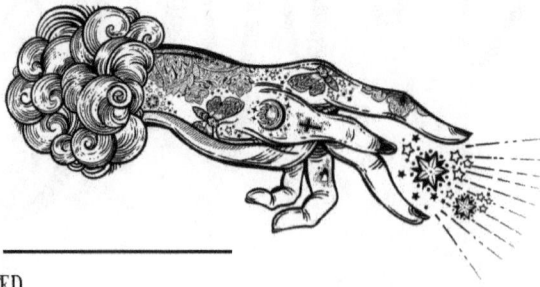

DATE _____

CASTER _____

RITUAL OR SPELL _____

PURPOSE _____

PARTICIPANTS _____

DEITIES INVOLVED _____

MANIFESTATION DATE _____

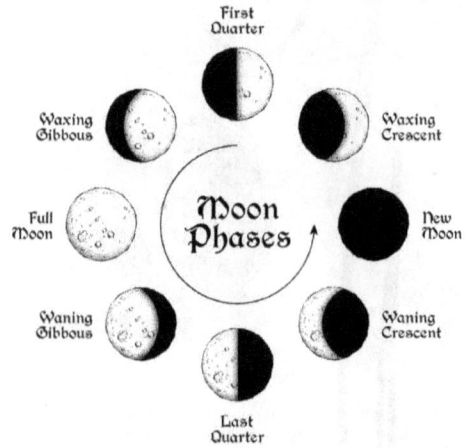

MOON PHASE _____

DESCRIPTION

FEELINGS & EFFECTS

INGREDIENTS & EQUIPMENT

_____

_____

_____

_____

_____

_____

"SO MOTE IT BE"

NoTES

NoTES

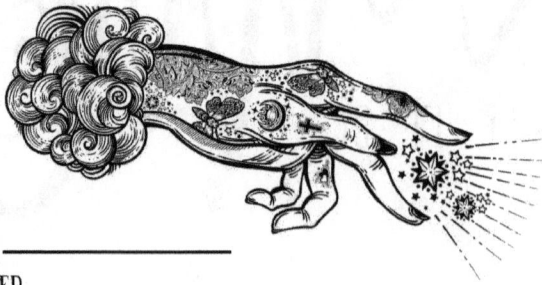

DATE _____

CASTER _____

RITUAL OR SPELL _____

PURPOSE _____

PARTICIPANTS _____

DEITIES INVOLVED _____

MANIFESTATION DATE _____

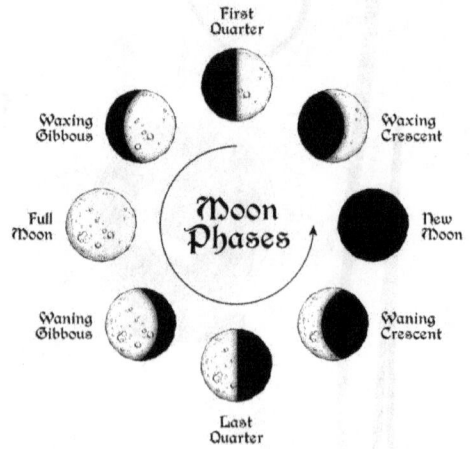

MOON PHASE _____

DESCRIPTION

FEELINGS & EFFECTS

INGREDIENTS & EQUIPMENT

_____

_____

_____

_____

_____

"So Mote It Be"

NOTES

NOTES

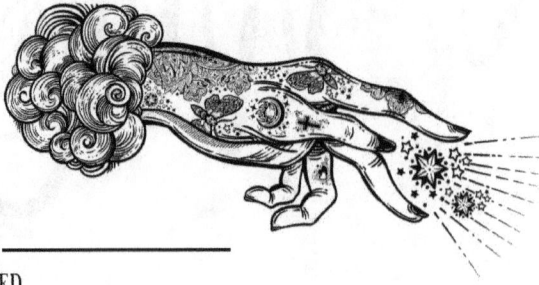

DATE _____

CASTER _____

RITUAL OR SPELL _____

PURPOSE _____

PARTICIPANTS _____

DEITIES INVOLVED _____

MANIFESTATION DATE _____

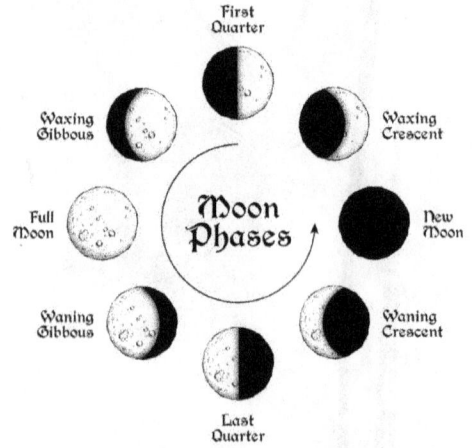

MOON PHASE _____

DESCRIPTION

FEELINGS & EFFECTS

INGREDIENTS & EQUIPMENT

_____

_____

_____

_____

_____

"So Mote It Be"

NOTES

NOTES

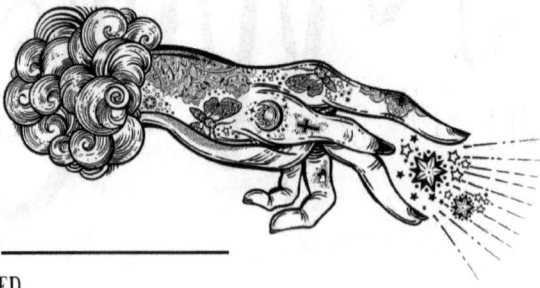

DATE _____

CASTER _____

RITUAL oR SPELL _____

PURPoSE _____

PARTICIPANTS _____

DEITIES INVoLVED _____

MANIFESTATION DATE _____

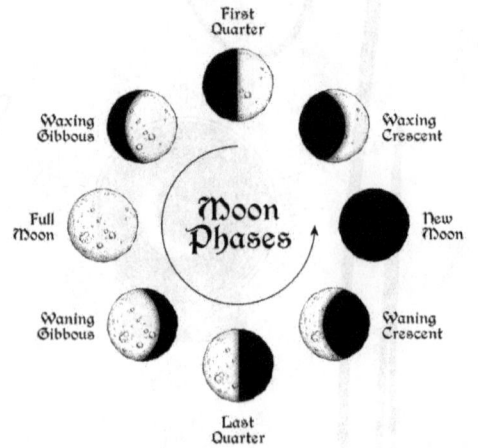

MOON PHASES

First Quarter

Waxing Gibbous

Waxing Crescent

Full Moon

New Moon

Waning Gibbous

Waning Crescent

Last Quarter

MOoN PHASE _____

DESCRIPTION

FEELINGS & EFFECTS

INGREDIENTS & EQUIPMENT

"So Mote It Be"

NoTES

NoTES

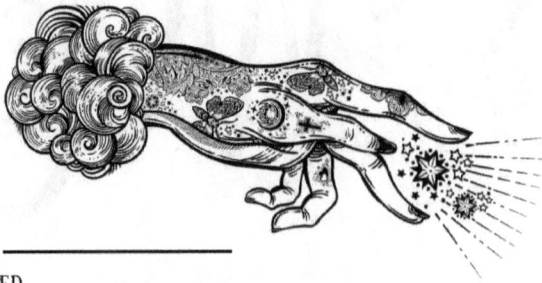

DATE _____

CASTER _____

RITUAL OR SPELL _____

PURPOSE _____

PARTICIPANTS _____

DEITIES INVOLVED _____

MANIFESTATION DATE _____

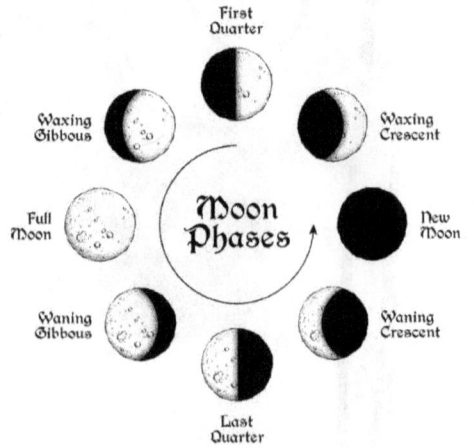

MOON PHASE _____

DESCRIPTION

FEELINGS & EFFECTS

INGREDIENTS & EQUIPMENT

_____

_____

_____

_____

_____

_____

"So Mote It Be"

NoTES

NoTES

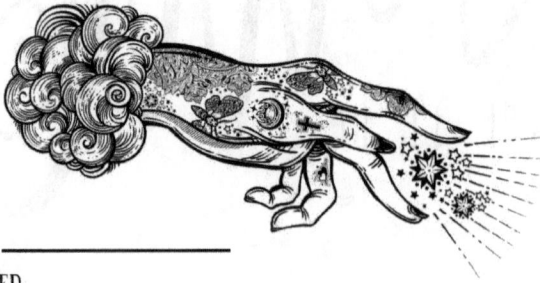

DATE _____

CASTER _____

RITUAL OR SPELL _____

PURPOSE _____

PARTICIPANTS _____

DEITIES INVOLVED _____

MANIFESTATION DATE _____

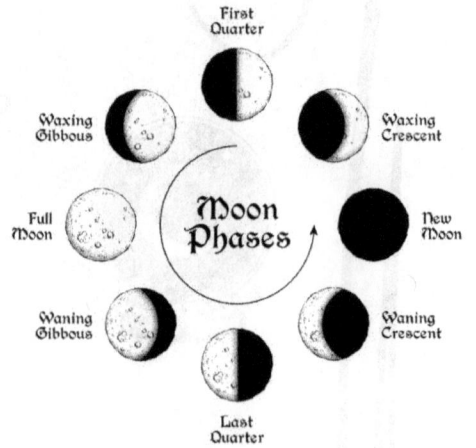

MOON PHASE _____

DESCRIPTION

FEELINGS & EFFECTS

INGREDIENTS & EQUIPMENT

_____

_____

_____

_____

_____

"So Mote It Be"

NOTES

NOTES

Dream

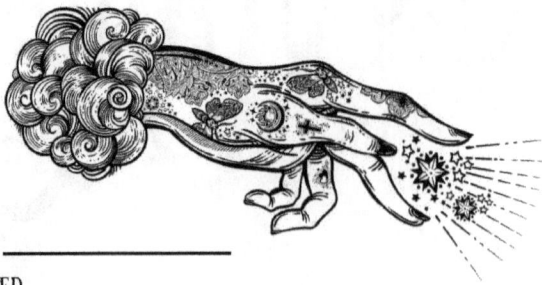

DATE _____

CASTER _____

RITUAL oR SPELL _____

PURPOSE _____

PARTICIPANTS _____

DEITIES INVOLVED _____

MANIFESTATION DATE _____

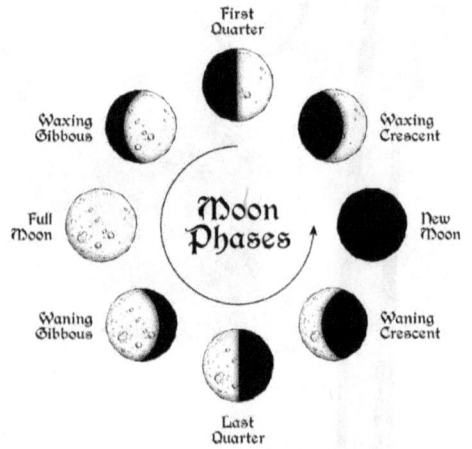

MOON PHASE _____

DESCRIPTION

FEELINGS & EFFECTS

INGREDIENTS & EQUIPMENT

_____

_____

_____

_____

_____

"So Mote It Be"

NOTES

NOTES

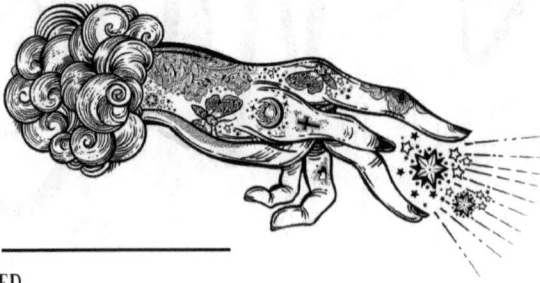

DATE _____

CASTER _____

RITUAL OR SPELL _____

PURPOSE _____

PARTICIPANTS _____

DEITIES INVOLVED _____

MANIFESTATION DATE _____

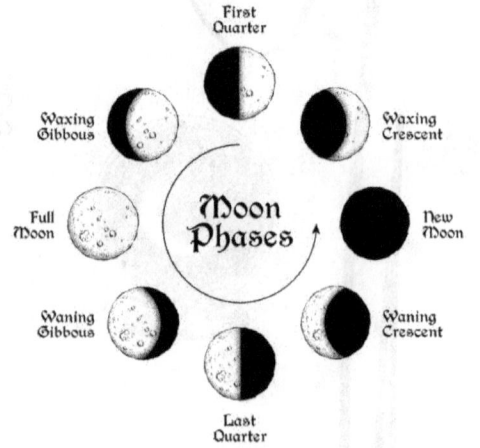

MOON PHASE _____

DESCRIPTION

FEELINGS & EFFECTS

INGREDIENTS & EQUIPMENT

_____

_____

_____

_____

_____

_____

"So Mote It Be"

NOTES

NOTES

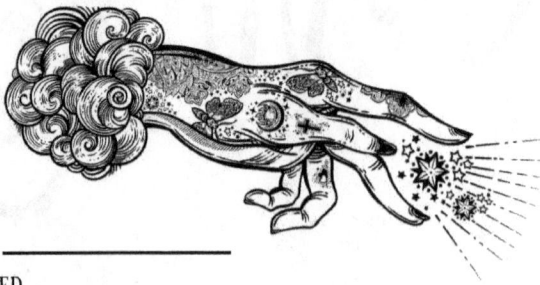

DATE _____

CASTER _____

RITUAL OR SPELL _____

PURPOSE _____

PARTICIPANTS _____

DEITIES INVOLVED _____

MANIFESTATION DATE _____

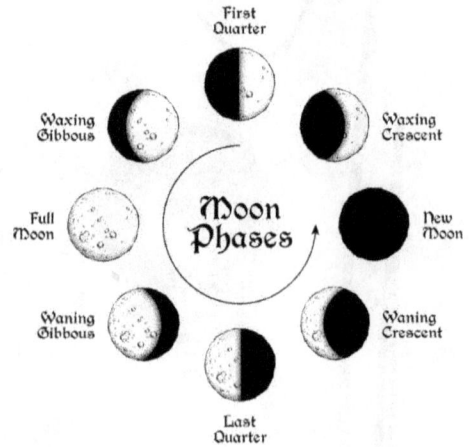

MOON PHASE _____

DESCRIPTION

FEELINGS & EFFECTS

INGREDIENTS & EQUIPMENT

_____

_____

_____

_____

_____

_____

"So Mote it be"

NOTES

NOTES

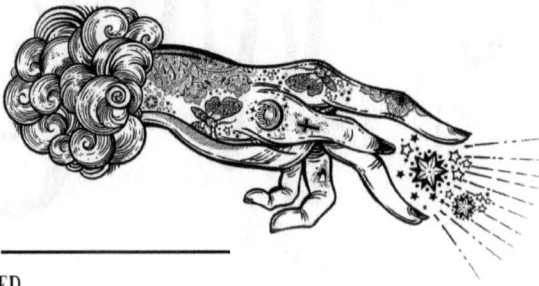

DATE _____

CASTER _____

RITUAL OR SPELL _____

PURPOSE _____

PARTICIPANTS _____

DEITIES INVOLVED _____

MANIFESTATION DATE _____

MOON PHASE _____

DESCRIPTION

FEELINGS & EFFECTS

INGREDIENTS & EQUIPMENT

"SO MOTE IT BE"

NOTES

NOTES

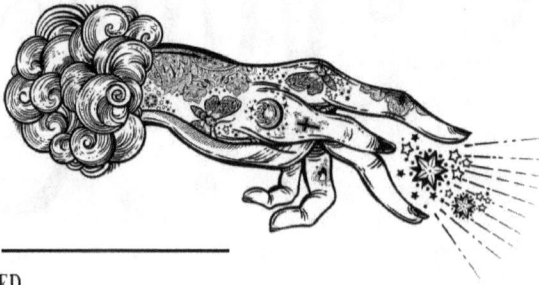

DATE _____

CASTER _____

RITUAL OR SPELL _____

PURPOSE _____

PARTICIPANTS _____

DEITIES INVOLVED _____

MANIFESTATION DATE _____

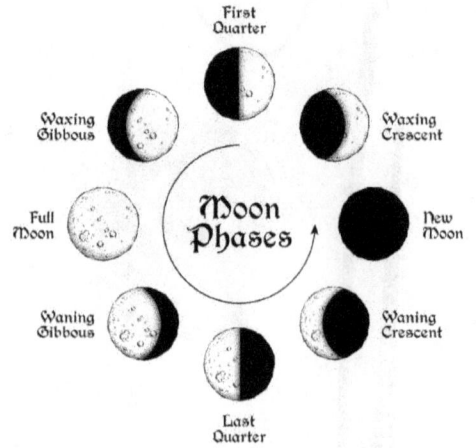

MOON PHASE _____

DESCRIPTION

FEELINGS & EFFECTS

INGREDIENTS & EQUIPMENT

_____

_____

_____

_____

_____

_____

"So Mote It Be"

NOTES

NOTES

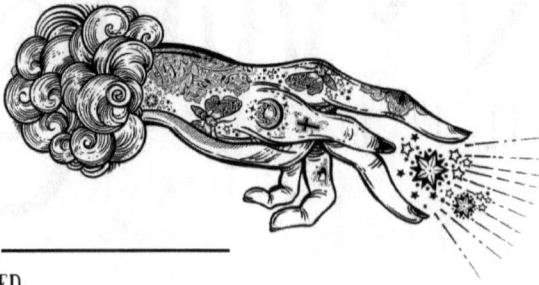

DATE _____

CASTER _____

RITUAL OR SPELL _____

PURPOSE _____

PARTICIPANTS _____

DEITIES INVOLVED _____

MANIFESTATION DATE _____

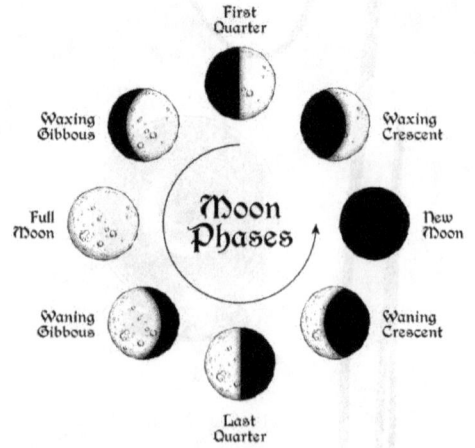

MOON PHASE _____

DESCRIPTION

FEELINGS & EFFECTS

INGREDIENTS & EQUIPMENT

_____

_____

_____

_____

_____

_____

"So Mote It Be"

NOTES

NOTES

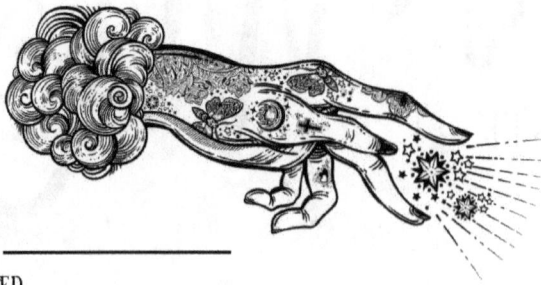

DATE _____

CASTER _____

RITUAL OR SPELL _____

PURPOSE _____

PARTICIPANTS _____

DEITIES INVOLVED _____

MANIFESTATION DATE _____

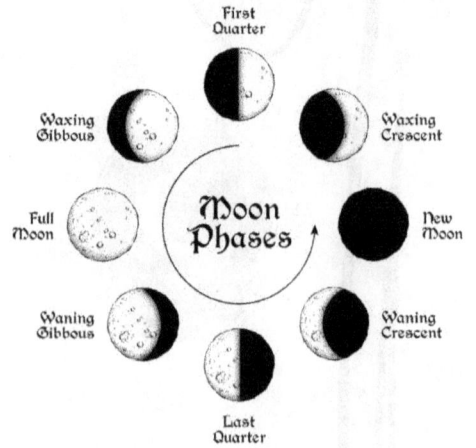

MOON PHASE _____

DESCRIPTION

FEELINGS & EFFECTS

INGREDIENTS & EQUIPMENT

_____

_____

_____

_____

_____

_____

"So Mote it be"

NoTES

NoTES

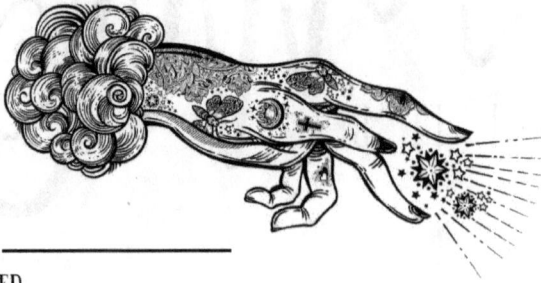

DATE _____

CASTER _____

RITUAL OR SPELL _____

PURPOSE _____

PARTICIPANTS _____

DEITIES INVOLVED _____

MANIFESTATION DATE _____

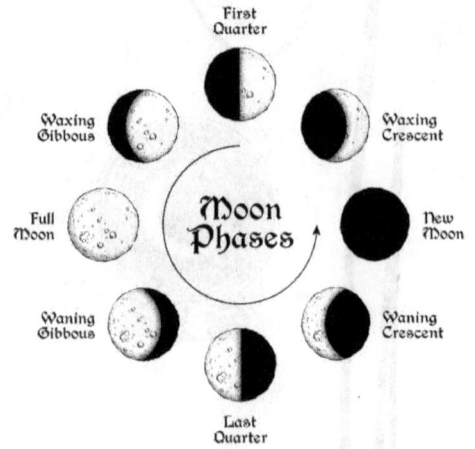

MOON PHASE _____

DESCRIPTION

FEELINGS & EFFECTS

INGREDIENTS & EQUIPMENT

_____

_____

_____

_____

_____

_____

"So Mote It Be"

NOTES

NOTES

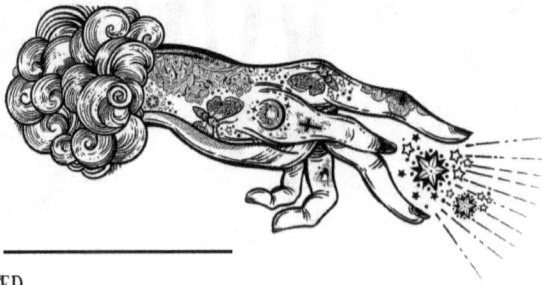

DATE _____

CASTER _____

RITUAL OR SPELL _____

PURPOSE _____

PARTICIPANTS _____

DEITIES INVOLVED _____

MANIFESTATION DATE _____

MOON PHASE _____

DESCRIPTION

INGREDIENTS & EQUIPMENT

_____

_____

_____

_____

_____

_____

FEELINGS & EFFECTS

"So Mote It Be"

NOTES

NOTES

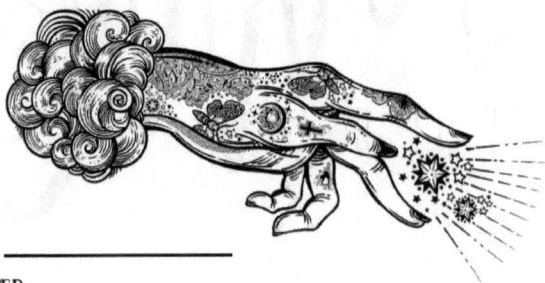

DATE _____

CASTER _____

RITUAL oR SPELL _____

PURPoSE _____

PARTICIPANTS _____

DEITIES INVOLVED _____

MANIFESTATION DATE _____

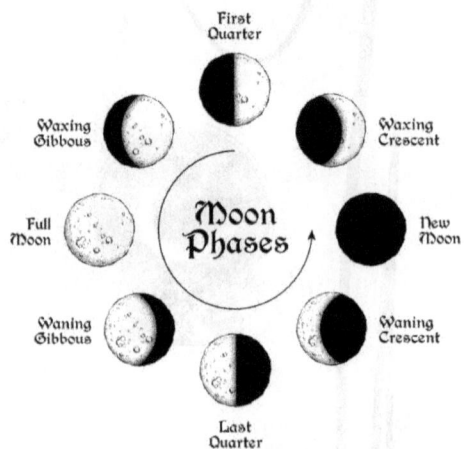

MooN PHASE _____

DESCRIPTION

FEELINGS & EFFECTS

INGREDIENTS & EQUIPMENT

_____

_____

_____

_____

_____

_____

"So Mote It Be"

NoTES

NoTES

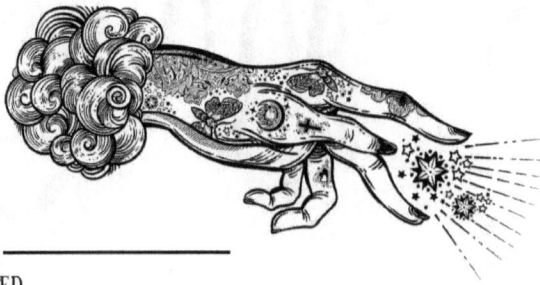

DATE _____

CASTER _____

RITUAL OR SPELL _____

PURPOSE _____

PARTICIPANTS _____

DEITIES INVOLVED _____

MANIFESTATION DATE _____

MOON PHASE _____

DESCRIPTION

FEELINGS & EFFECTS

INGREDIENTS & EQUIPMENT

_____

_____

_____

_____

_____

_____

"So Mote It Be"

NoTES

NoTES

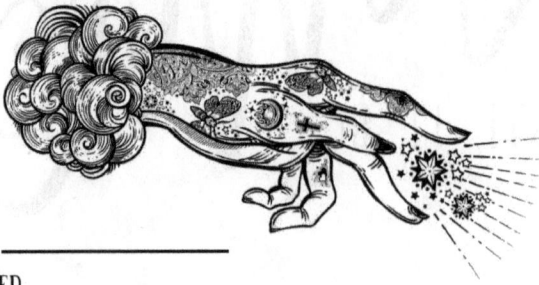

DATE _____

CASTER _____

RITUAL OR SPELL _____

PURPOSE _____

PARTICIPANTS _____

DEITIES INVOLVED _____

MANIFESTATION DATE _____

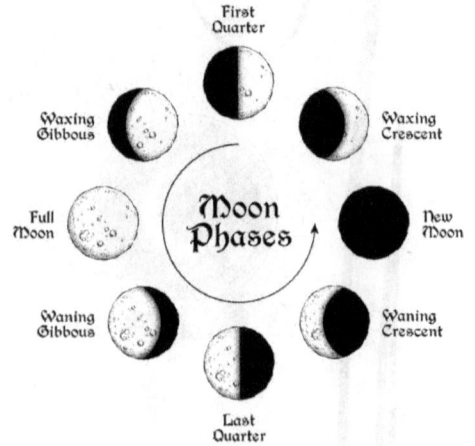

MOON PHASE _____

DESCRIPTION

FEELINGS & EFFECTS

INGREDIENTS & EQUIPMENT

"So Mote It Be"

NOTES

NOTES

Manifestations

Name of Spell	Casting Date	Manifestation Date

Manifestations

Name of Spell	Casting Date	Manifestation Date

Manifestations

Name of Spell	Casting Date	Manifestation Date

Manifestations

Name of Spell	Casting Date	Manifestation Date